Publisher: So Amazing Publications
Email: soamazingpublications@gmail.com

ISBN: 9798327095724

If you are a content creator or suppo me, please share this book on social media and tag #soamazingpublications #authortiffanyf

Thank you for your support!

Table of Contents

Introduction

Welcome to your journey as a content creator! This guide is designed to not only provide you with practical tips but also to keep you motivated and inspired. Content creation can be challenging, but it's also incredibly rewarding. Let's dive in and make your creative journey a fun and fulfilling one!

Chapter 1: Discover Your Passion

Fun Tip: Passion Board

Create a "Passion Board" using a large poster or digital tool like Pinterest. Fill it with images, quotes, and ideas that inspire you. Refer to this board whenever you need a burst of inspiration or a reminder of why you started.

Chapter 2: Setting Up Your Space

Fun Tip: Personalized Workspace

Make your workspace a place you love. Add fun decorations, inspirational quotes, and everything you need within arm's reach. A cozy and personalized workspace can boost your creativity and productivity.

Chapter 3: Finding Your Unique Voice

Fun Tip: Voice Journal

Start a "Voice Journal" where you jot down ideas, phrases, and themes that resonate with you. Experiment with different styles and see what feels most authentic. Your unique voice is what will set you apart.

Chapter 4: Creating a Content Plan

Fun Tip: Content Calendar Party

Host a "Content Calendar Party" with fellow creators. Plan out your content for the next month while enjoying snacks and drinks. Sharing ideas can spark new inspiration and make planning fun.

Chapter 5: Developing Your Brand

Fun Tip: Mood Board

Create a "Brand Mood Board" that reflects the colors, fonts, and images that define your brand. This visual representation will help you stay consistent and inspired.

Chapter 6: Engaging with Your Audience

Fun Tip: Audience Polls

Use polls and Q&A sessions to interact with your audience. This not only engages them but also gives you insights into what they want to see more of.

Chapter 7: Mastering Different Platforms

Fun Tip: Platform Challenge

Challenge yourself to create content for a platform you've never used before. This can help you discover new skills and reach different audiences.

Chapter 8: Consistency is Key

Fun Tip: Content Streak

Set a content streak goal, like posting every day for a month. Reward yourself with a treat or a fun activity when you reach your goal.

Chapter 9: Leveraging Analytics

Fun Tip: Data Dive

Make a game out of your analytics. See which posts performed best and try to identify patterns. This can turn a mundane task into an exciting discovery process.

Chapter 10: Collaborating with Others

Fun Tip: Collaboration Bingo

Create a "Collaboration Bingo" card with different types of collaborations (guest posts, interviews, joint videos, etc.). Try to complete a row for a fun and engaging way to expand your network.

Chapter 11: Monetizing Your Content

Fun Tip: Earnings Tracker

So Amazing
PUBLICATIONS

Use a fun and colorful tracker to monitor your earnings. Watching your progress can be motivating and visually rewarding.

Chapter 12: Staying Inspired

Fun Tip: Inspiration Jar

Keep an "Inspiration Jar" filled with ideas, quotes, and challenges. Whenever you feel stuck, pull out a slip of paper for a quick boost of creativity.

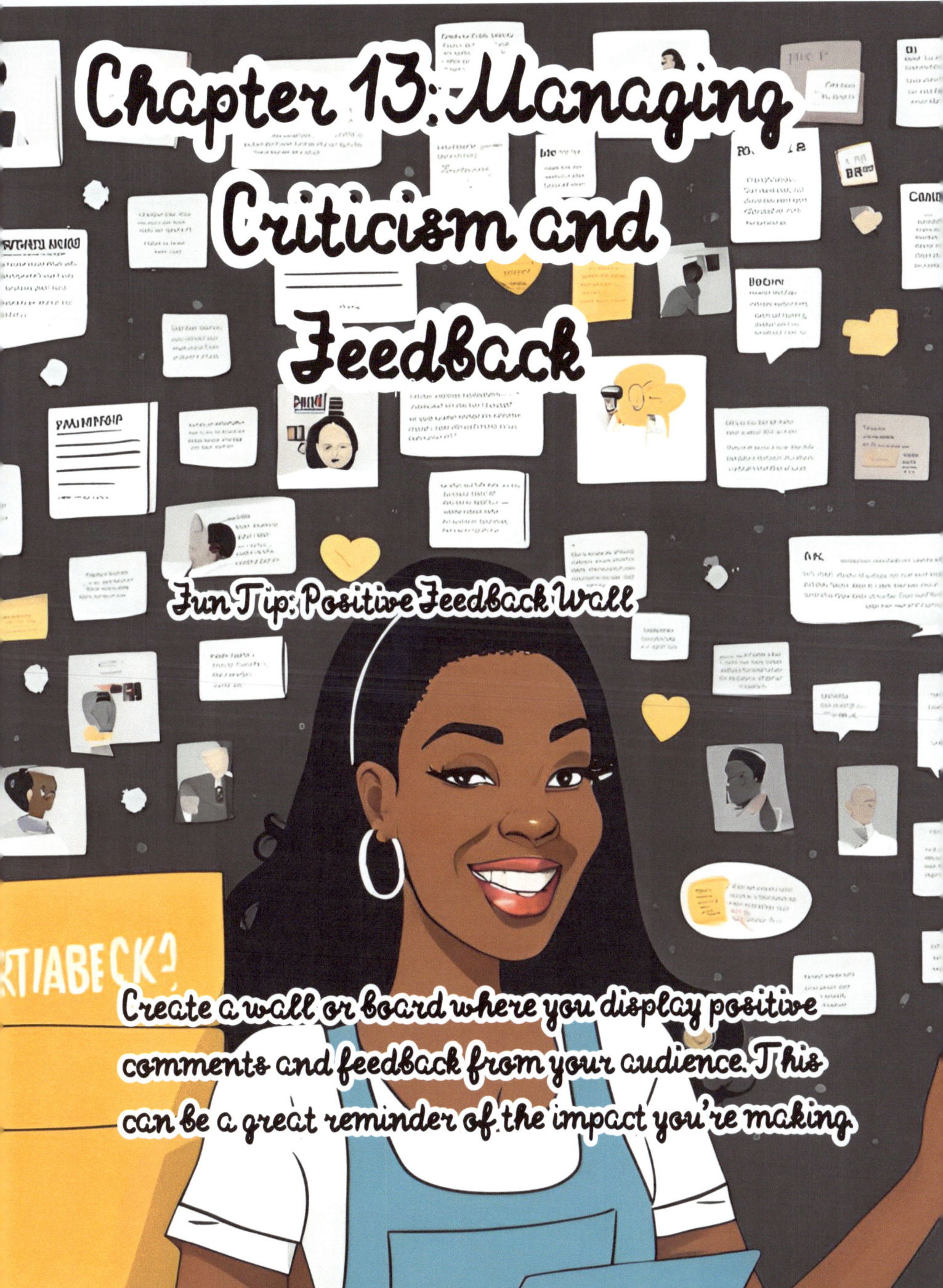

Chapter 13: Managing Criticism and Feedback

Fun Tip: Positive Feedback Wall

Create a wall or board where you display positive comments and feedback from your audience. This can be a great reminder of the impact you're making.

Chapter 14: Expanding Your Skills

Fun Tip: Skill Swap

Partner with another creator to swap skills. Teach each other something new, whether it's video editing, graphic design, or writing techniques.

Chapter 15: Balancing Content Creation and Life

Fun Tip: Time Blocks

Use colorful time blocks in your planner to allocate time for content creation and personal activities. Visual balance can help you manage your time effectively.

Chapter 16: Dealing with Burnout

Fun Tip: Self-Care Routine

Create a fun self-care routine that includes activities you love. Schedule regular breaks and pamper sessions to recharge your creative energy.

Chapter 17: Legal and Ethical Considerations

Fun Tip: Legal Checklist

Make a checklist of legal and ethical considerations for your content. Turn it into a game by seeing how quickly you can complete each task correctly.

Chapter 18: Adapting to Trends

Fun Tip: Trend Tracker

Keep a "Trend Tracker" to note down emerging trends. Try to predict what's next and how you can incorporate it into your content.

Chapter 19: Celebrating Milestones

Fun Tip: Celebration Jar

Whenever you reach a milestone, write it down and put it in a "Celebration Jar". Open the jar at the end of the year to see all your achievements.

Chapter 20: Building a Legacy

Fun Tip: Legacy Time Capsule

Create a digital or physical "Legacy Time Capsule." Fill it with your favorite pieces of content, messages to your future self, and your goals and dreams as a content creator. Set a date a few years in the future to open it and reflect on your journey. This can be a powerful reminder of how far you've come and keep you motivated to continue building your

Conclusion

Congratulations on completing this guide! Remember, the journey of a content creator is a marathon, not a sprint. Keep having fun, stay motivated, and continue to share your unique voice with the world. Happy creating!

About the Author

Tiffany Forbes resides in Petersburg, Virginia. She holds a BA in English from Virginia State University and a Master's degree in Human Services, specializing in social and community services, from Capella University. She is also a QMHP-A and studied at Duke University to become a Tobacco Treatment Specialist.

Tiffany is the founder of So Amazing Publications, a small but prolific publishing company. As an author, she writes in various genres, including urban fiction, romance, and sci-fi. Her debut indie novel, *Silly of Me: May the Best Woman Win*, was released in February 2016. Currently, she is working on several projects, so stay tuned for exciting new releases.

In addition to her writing career, Tiffany works full-time in mental health and is a content creator on social media platforms like Facebook, Instagram, and TikTok. She focuses on self-care and advocates for health wellness and smoke-free living. Don't forget to like, follow, and subscribe to the exclusive email list.

Reviews Matter

Hello! My goal is to build relationships with my readers. I strive to send out newsletters with details about new releases, special offers, and exciting things with So Amazing Publications.

I would appreciate a few minutes of your time if you could leave a brief review on the book's Amazon page.

Like and Follow on Social Media

Website: Soamazingpublications.com

Facebook: Facebook.com/soamazuingpublications.com

Twitter: https://twitter.com/authortiffanyf

Instagram: https://www.instagram.comauthortiffanyf